BLOOMSBURY
CHILDREN'S
BOOKS

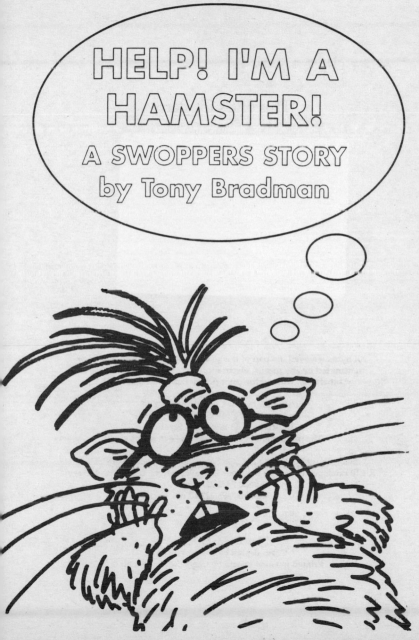

HELP! I'M A HAMSTER!

A SWOPPERS STORY
by Tony Bradman

This one's for Barry

First published in Great Britain in 1996
Text copyright © 1996 Tony Bradman
Illustrations © 1996 Clive Scruton
The moral right of the author has been asserted

Bloomsbury Publishing PLC, 38 Soho Square, London W1V 5DF
A CIP catalogue record for this book is available from The British Library
ISBN 0 7475 2273 1 hb
ISBN 0 7475 2272 3 pb

10 9 8 7 6 5

Text design by AB3
Cover design by Alison Withey
Printed in Great Britain by Clays Ltd, St Ives plc

Contents

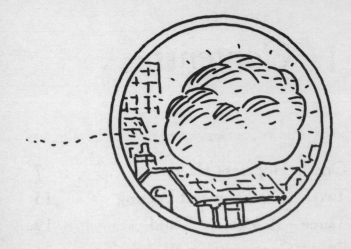

A small cloud of gas drifts towards a quiet street...
It shimmers, and gives off an eerie glow.
Where it came from is a mystery. Perhaps it
seeped from the depths of the Earth.
Perhaps it is the product of a secret laboratory...
Whatever the truth, one thing is certain. Any
child who meets it is in for an amazing experience,
as a particular girl is about to discover.
Follow her as she tumbles into the weird, wild
and wonderful world of... **Swoppers!**

CHAPTER ONE
Hopeless Harry

'Please, Harry,' said Alice Buggins, desperately. She was lying flat on the floor of her best friend Sophie Farr's bedroom, talking to Sophie's pet hamster. 'I'm begging you. Don't just sit there – *do* something.'

But Harry wouldn't budge. He stayed hunched over in the middle of the carpet, a small ball of orange fur with pink paws and beady black eyes.

'Maybe we ought to let him have a rest, Alice,' said Sophie, anxiously. 'He's been out of his cage for ages. He's probably getting tired.'

'Tired?' said Alice, sitting up. 'He hasn't *done* anything yet. Listen, Harry, don't you realise how important this is? You're our only chance. We'll never win that prize unless you start showing some talent!'

Alice could hardly believe her favourite TV programme was coming to town this Saturday. She and Sophie usually watched *The Kids Rule OK! Roadshow* together – and now they might actually be on it.

The presenter was called Johnny Dee, and Alice thought he was really funny. If he liked a new song or video, he always said *'Wow, knock-out!'*, threw his arms wide, then fell over backwards.

But the most exciting thing was the prize he'd announced for this week's Pet Talent Contest, the start of every show – a trip for two with *The Roadshow* to Wonderworld, the best theme park in Florida!

Alice adored theme parks, and Wonderworld was the one she'd always wanted to see. So she was determined to win. She didn't have a pet, but she had persuaded Sophie they should try to get Harry into the contest.

Harry, however, had turned out to be... hopeless. They had been working with him for a week, but all he wanted to do was eat and sleep. And time was ticking away. *The Roadshow* was due to arrive tomorrow.

Sophie was having second thoughts as well.

'Look, Alice,' she was saying. 'I'm not sure about this. Harry's always been nervous, and going on TV might be too much for him. I mean, there's bound to be a big crowd for *The Roadshow*, and it's pretty noisy...'

'Stop worrying, Sophie,' said Alice, firmly. Sophie could be as nervous as a hamster herself, and sometimes Alice had to be tough with her. 'He'll be fine. Let's play him that tape again, OK? Sophie, what's the matter?'

Alice had noticed Sophie wasn't paying her any attention.

'You didn't shut the door properly,' said Sophie, sounding panicky.

'Didn't I?' said Alice, glancing over her shoulder.

The bedroom door *was* slightly ajar, and just then, someone on the landing pushed it further open. Someone with whiskers, a mangled ear, and a single mean, yellow eye. It was Sinbad, the Farr family cat.

He was sly and rather smelly, and Alice knew he often killed mice and other small creatures. He had a habit of leaving their heads by the back door, and messy bits of their insides scattered round the garden.

Alice also knew Sinbad had been after Harry since the day Sophie had got him. What happened next, therefore,

wasn't a surprise. Sinbad leapt, Harry sat transfixed
with horror, and Sophie dived headlong to the rescue.

'Oh no you don't!' she yelled, saving Harry from
Sinbad's sharp claws. She popped her pet in his cage,
then turned to glare at the cat. Sinbad slunk off with a
'Drat! Foiled again!' expression on his face.

'Hey, that was terrific!' laughed Alice. 'It was just
like something from *Tom and Jerry*. And it's given me a
brilliant idea! We could take Harry *and* Sinbad along as
a double act, let them go
on the stage and...'

'Over my dead body,' snarled Sophie, hugging Harry's cage.

'Er... just kidding, Sophie,' said Alice, realising she might have gone a little too far. She had actually been serious, but she couldn't risk spooking her friend into pulling out of the Pet Talent Contest now.

Alice would have to make do with Harry alone. Still, what was it her Dad said about competitions? *You've got to be in 'em to win 'em.* And Alice was a born optimist. She was convinced something would turn up.

It did. But Alice could never, *ever* have imagined what it would be...

CHAPTER TWO
The Strangest Feeling

Alice set the alarm clock to wake her early the next morning. She jumped out of bed as soon as it beep-beeped, and dashed straight into the bathroom. She didn't want to waste a second of this extra-special day.

Sophie's parents were driving Sophie and Harry to the park where *The Roadshow* would be taking place. Alice's parents had said they'd like to come along, so Alice was going with them, and meeting Sophie there.

At least, that was how they'd arranged it the night

before. But when Alice went into the dining room for breakfast, she found her Mum and Dad slumped at the table, looking pale and unhappy.

'I'm sorry, love,' said Alice's Dad. 'We both seem to have a tummy bug. I don't think we'll be moving very far from the house today.'

'I won't be moving very far from the loo, actually,' said Alice's Mum, leaving the kitchen as fast as she could shuffle in her slippers.

'That's OK,' said Alice. 'I can go with Sophie and her parents.'

'You're probably right,' said Alice's Dad, rising unsteadily to his feet. 'But I'd better phone to make sure they haven't left already...'

'There's no need, Dad,' said Alice, finishing her cereal. 'They won't have. Catch you later! Hope you and Mum feel better!'

'So do I...' said Dad, and waved, feebly.

Alice shut the front door behind her and cheerfully set off. Sophie's house was just round the corner. As there were no roads to cross, Alice was almost always allowed to walk to Sophie's by herself.

There was no one else in the street. Alice, however, didn't notice it was empty and oddly quiet, even for this early on a Saturday. She was too busy trying to work out a way of winning that trip to Wonderworld.

She decided at last that she should simply *focus* on

Harry. Then she might think of something interesting he could do. So Alice concentrated until images of her best friend's hamster completely filled her mind...

...And at that precise moment, a certain small cloud of gas drifted up, silently wrapping Alice in its shimmering coils. She stopped, stunned by the eerily glowing

mist that had surrounded her.

Then she got the strangest feeling in her stomach, and for an instant she wondered if she had the same tummy bug as her Mum and Dad. She'd had bugs in the past, though, and this seemed... different.

It felt as if her own stomach was trying to swallow her.

There was no other way to describe it. Every part of her body was being sucked in towards her middle. Alice suddenly bent double, fell to the ground, rolled on her back, and pulled her knees to her chest.

She moaned, and she groaned, and she gritted her teeth. The sucking grew stronger, and stronger, and stronger, and Alice thought that if it went on much longer, she wouldn't be able to stand it any more.

Eventually, something seemed to *SNAP!* inside her, and a *WHOOSH-ING!* sensation followed. Alice could have sworn she flew into the air and whizzed crazily around, like a balloon you blow up and let go.

This can't be happening, she thought, just as she *CRASHED!* into something hard, which jarred her from top to bottom.

Then the most terrible tingling began in her toes... raced up her legs... flowed over her body... crackled up her

neck... tickled her cheeks... made her nose go *POP!* and finally her ears go... *PING!* and *PING!*

Alice closed her eyes. She was as dazed and dizzy as if she'd just been on a wild roller-coaster, and she knew she had to get herself under control. She stayed still, and gradually the dizziness started to fade.

She realised she was lying on her back, with her head propped against something. She couldn't feel any pain, but she *did* feel very peculiar.

She opened her eyes and peered down at her body.

Alice saw a lot of orange fur and four pink paws. She couldn't take it in at first, and blinked a couple of times. Then the awful truth hit her.

'*HELP!*' she screamed. '*I'M A HAMSTER!*'

CHAPTER THREE
A Massive Thud

Alice screamed and screamed and screamed, and then she paused. 'This *has* to be a nightmare,' she said. 'If I pinch myself, I'll wake up.'

But that was easier said than done. Hamster paws aren't much good for pinching with, and after a few clumsy tries, Alice realised she wasn't getting anywhere. If this *was* a nightmare, she was stuck in it.

Alice struggled onto all fours. As she did so, she caught a glimpse of shimmering mist, and remembered that weird cloud of gas. It seemed to be drifting slowly over a roof and away from the street.

And what had happened to the street? Everything in it – the houses, the cars, the lamp posts – was huge, fifty times bigger than normal.

'I don't think I like the look of this,' Alice muttered uneasily. 'Maybe something seriously weird *is* going on...'

After all, she *had* been thinking about Harry when the cloud appeared. Suppose it was poisonous, or even radioactive, and somehow transformed people into whatever was in their minds when it touched them?

Alice let that sink in... then decided to start screaming again.

But suddenly she heard a massive *THUD!* and felt the ground shake beneath her. Another *THUD!* followed, and another, and another, and with each *THUD!* a shockwave seemed to pass through the pavement.

She looked round, and saw a giant striding towards her.

Alice's jaw dropped. It was... *the postman!*

The *THUDS!* were his colossal shoes crashing on the flagstones as he came nearer and nearer. He was whistling loudly, a sound that pierced Alice's brain and made her wince, and he obviously hadn't seen her.

Alice thought that was probably because she was tucked under an overgrown hedge next to a gate-post. She also realised it must have been the gate-post that had ended her crazy whizzing around.

And that the gate attached to it was... Sophie's!

A massive shoe stamped to a halt millimetres from Alice's snout, making her jump. The postman opened

the gate and went through. He strode down the path like a walking skyscraper, *THUD! THUD! THUD!*

Alice scampered in behind him. She dashed for the shelter of a bush, nestled in its leaves and peered out. She watched the postman stuff several giant letters through Sophie's front door, then turn and *THUD!* off.

Alice knew now this definitely *wasn't* a dream.

It was just too real. Alice had been amazed by the sensation of running on all fours. She had felt her paws pattering on the path, and the wind whipping through her whiskers. She had felt her fur prickling with fear.

And the thing that had frightened her most was being exposed.

Hiding in the bush made her feel a little safer, but certainly not safe enough. Alice had an overwhelming urge to be *inside* Sophie's house.

In any case, Alice badly needed help, and the nearest people who might be able to give her some were Sophie and her parents.

The question was – how could she get in?

She couldn't reach the button for the bell, and she couldn't knock. But she couldn't wait till Sophie or her parents opened the front door and came out, either. No, Alice had to do something, and she had to do it now.

Perhaps the back door was open, she thought. It was worth a try...

Alice emerged cautiously from her hiding place. She scuttled across a flower bed, shot down the passage beside the house, and skidded to a stop on the patio, beneath the barbecue. The back door was closed.

But it *did* have a cat flap.

Alice didn't think twice. She took a deep breath, started running, launched herself into the air... and crashed through. She landed on the mat, rolled over a couple of times, and finished in a heap.

Alice scrambled onto her paws. She shook her head to clear it. Then a large, dark shadow fell over her, and she froze on the spot.

'Oh, I say,' purred an evil voice. 'What a *spectacular* entrance!'

Alice turned, and found herself looking up at... *Sinbad!*

CHAPTER FOUR

Conversation
With a Cat

It was definitely him, although like the postman, Sinbad was gigantic, a cat the size of a double-decker bus. That was strange enough, thought Alice. But was she totally mad, or had she heard him speak, too?

'Excuse me,' she said, confused. 'Did you just... *say* something?'

'I certainly did,' replied Sinbad, edging closer. 'Mind you, that entrance of yours almost left me speechless, Harry old chap. I must admit I never thought you were the athletic type. You've always seemed rather lazy.'

'Hang on a minute,' spluttered Alice. 'What did you call me?'

'And I can't imagine *what* you were doing in the garden,' Sinbad continued, ignoring her question. 'Not that it matters. The important point is that you're here. I'm *so* glad to see you outside that ghastly cage again.'

'Listen, er... Sinbad,' said Alice. 'This is hard to explain... I don't understand it myself. But something

weird has happened to me, and I need help. I can say one thing, though. I'm not who you think I am.'

'Oh, Harry, what a little tease you are!' Sinbad scolded, edging closer still. 'You'll be telling me next you're not even a hamster.'

'I'm not, actually,' said Alice, suddenly feeling impatient. She didn't have time for a conversation with a *cat*, for heaven's sake! 'I'm Alice Buggins, Sophie's best friend, and if you don't mind, I'll be on my way...'

'So soon?' said Sinbad, casually placing a huge paw directly in her path. 'And just as we were finally beginning to get acquainted. You know, you look like a hamster to me. You'll probably taste like a hamster, too...'

Alice's fur instantly stood on end, and she went cold all over.

There was absolutely no mistaking Sinbad's intention. His mean yellow eye was firmly fixed on her, and filled with a hot and hungry gleam.

Of course, *Alice* knew she was a human being who had been turned into a hamster by accident. But Sinbad obviously thought she was the small, completely defenceless creature he'd been after for ages.

A picture of the gory fate she was facing flashed into Alice's mind. It would be like the worst scene from a horror movie for grown-ups, she thought, all slashing and biting and blood spurting everywhere.

Alice realised she had to do something, and she had to do it quickly.

'Are you quite sure about that?' she said, trying to peer past Sinbad for an escape route. But he had cleverly boxed her into a corner, and was blocking the view. 'I've heard us hamsters taste pretty awful.'

'You're too modest,' purred Sinbad. 'Now, shall we get on with it?'

'No, wait!' squealed Alice as Sinbad prepared to pounce. She had just had an idea that might buy her some time. 'Er... I thought you cats liked to play with your prey first,' she said. 'How about a bit of a chase?'

'Why, Harry!' said Sinbad, surprised. 'You really are a changed hamster. What a wonderfully adventurous suggestion. Yes, that might be fun.'

'I expect you to give me a start, though,' said Alice.

'Very well,' said Sinbad. 'I'll count to... ten.'

'*Ten?*' squeaked Alice, outraged. 'But that's not fair!'

'I think you'll find life generally isn't, Harry,' said Sinbad. 'I tell you what, though. I won't start counting until you're off and running, agreed?'

'Oh, all right,' tutted Alice. She had been hoping for a lot more. 'And look, I want to get something straight here and now. I am *not* Harry, OK?'

'Don't worry,' whispered Sinbad. 'It's none of my business if you slipped out of the house when you shouldn't have, you old devil. Your secret is safe with me. In fact, I doubt if anyone will ever know...'

'I give up,' muttered Alice. Sinbad glanced at her

sharply. 'No, I don't mean it like that,' she added, hurriedly. 'You've still got to chase me. Ready...' Alice paused. 'You'll have to step aside,' she said.

'I suppose I will, won't I?' sighed Sinbad.

He moved reluctantly, and Alice got her first proper sight of the whole kitchen. The smooth, shiny floor stretched into the distance. And there wasn't a single hiding place between her and the door in the far wall.

Maybe a chase wasn't such a good idea, she thought...

CHAPTER FIVE

Run... or Die!

Alice realised there was no getting out of it, though. It was run, or die horribly, then and there. Suddenly, a wave of anger surged through her. She wasn't going to let a one-eyed, smelly old cat beat *her*.

She certainly wasn't going to let him *eat* her, either.

Alice also realised every extra second she could grab was vital to her survival. Time for some cheating, she thought, and smiled, inwardly...

'Steady...' she said. Sinbad nodded, and crouched like a sprinter at the starting line. Then Alice... *didn't* say the word he was waiting to hear.

Instead, she simply shot off as fast as her short legs would carry her.

'Naughty, naughty,' Sinbad called out. 'Didn't you forget to say go, you rascal? Oh well... *Onetwothreefourfivesixseveneightnineten!*' he said, rattling through the numbers. 'Ready or not, here I come!'

Alice put her head down and frantically tried to speed up. But running across the kitchen floor turned out to be rather hard. In fact, Alice's little pink hamster paws just couldn't get a grip on the slippery surface.

It was like running on ice, and that door seemed as distant as ever...

'Yikes!' squealed Alice, as Sinbad loomed beside her.

'Come on, Harry, you can do better than that, can't you?' he said as he trotted along. 'I don't call this much of a chase. You're so *slow*.'

'At least... I'm not... as *ugly* as you,' panted Alice, and swerved away.

'Really, Harry,' said Sinbad, sounding slightly offended. 'There's no need to get personal. We're supposed to be having fun. Now I'll just wait over there, and in the mean time, I suggest you consider an apology.'

'Not... in a... million years,' panted Alice, defiantly.

Sinbad didn't reply. He padded ahead, his easy stride taking him swiftly to the door. He sat by it, and cleaned his claws while he waited for Alice to arrive. She slowed down, her anger boiling inside her.

This wasn't much like *Tom and Jerry*, she thought bitterly.

Alice reached the wall at last and stopped, out of breath. She noticed the door was open a crack. She could see the edge of the thick hall carpet, and an expanse of darkness beyond. She thought about making a dash...

But Sinbad was watching her with a very smug look on his face. Alice racked her brains for some way of escaping him, although she had a nasty, sinking feeling that she was completely in his power.

'No apology, then?' asked Sinbad. Alice stayed fiercely silent. 'I must say I'm disappointed, Harry. Still, you're forgiven. I'm sure this has all been something of a strain for you. Never mind, it will soon be over...'

Sinbad advanced confidently. Alice shrunk back. She wanted to close her eyes, but she couldn't take them off the cat's wickedly sharp teeth, and the giant pink tongue that lolled out of his mouth, dripping with spit.

This looked like the end for Alice... but suddenly, the door opened and hit Sinbad – *THUNK!* – square on the head! In the split second before he was swept aside, Alice saw he looked nearly knocked out.

Now *that* was more like *Tom and Jerry*, she thought, and giggled.

Alice also realised doors don't usually open by themselves. So she wasn't surprised when two huge trainers *THUMPED!* into the kitchen, one after the other. A pair of giant legs in jeans rose high above them.

And the legs belonged to... Sophie's Dad!

He was moving towards the back door, obviously unaware of what had happened to Sinbad. Alice didn't care about that. She thought the cat deserved all he got. Sophie's Dad hadn't noticed *her*, though!

She *had* to attract his attention!

But before Alice could do anything, he crossed the

kitchen in three giant steps, pulled open the back door... and was gone.

'Bother!' said Alice.

She couldn't possibly catch up with him. Besides, she didn't want to be outside again. Not that it was much safer indoors, she realised, wondering how long she had before Sinbad recovered and came after her.

Better not hang around to find out, she decided, and ran into the hall...

CHAPTER SIX
Hell-Hole for Hamsters

Alice scuttled over the carpet. She was relieved to discover it was a lot easier to run on than the smooth kitchen floor. The hall was smaller and darker too, and the further Alice got from Sinbad, the happier she felt.

To her left was the cluttered space under the stairs where the Farr family kept their coats, shoes, bags and umbrellas. They were all gigantic, of course, but Alice was beginning to get used to that.

To her right was the wall separating the hall from the other downstairs rooms. There was a dining room and a front room, and Alice could see that both doors were shut. She wondered if Sophie were behind one.

Alice had decided Sophie was her best bet. Most people would probably pass out if a hamster spoke to them, but Alice knew Sophie wouldn't. Even so, it would be very hard to explain... and Alice still had to find her.

Suddenly Alice glimpsed a strange object ahead. It was a huge box made out of shiny bars. As Alice approached, she realised it was Harry's cage. He was inside it, holding the bars and staring intently at her.

'Who are *you?*' he said. 'And what are you doing out there?'

Alice was only mildly taken aback that Harry had spoken, and that she could understand him. After all, she had discovered she could speak fluent cat – so why shouldn't she be able to speak hamster, too?

'Actually, Harry, it's a long story, and I don't think I've got time to tell it at the moment,' Alice replied, glancing nervously over her shoulder. 'Listen, do you know where Sophie is? This is a matter of life or death.'

'Do you mean the human who's supposed to look after me?' said Harry.

'Yes, I do,' said Alice, eagerly. 'I need to...'

'Huh!' snorted Harry. 'Don't talk to me about *her*, or that other one she's always with. They've done nothing but torture me for the last week. I'm exhausted, totally exhausted. It's more than a hamster can bear!'

'Oh, come on, Harry,' said Alice. 'It wasn't *that* bad.'

'How do you know what it was like?' said Harry.

'Er... I don't,' said Alice, wishing she'd kept her mouth shut.

'Well, then,' said Harry. 'Believe me, it's been *awful*. I just want to be left alone to eat and sleep like any ordinary hamster...'

Harry went on and on, listing the things they had made him do, like jumping through hoops and tackling obstacle courses. Alice almost felt guilty, and avoided his gaze. Then something he'd said made her think.

Harry wanted to be left *alone*, did he? But what if he wasn't alone the next time Sophie looked into his cage? What if she saw a *second* hamster with him? A second hamster who was absolutely *identical* to her pet?

Now Alice was this close to Harry, she could see why Sinbad had mistaken her for him. The hall mirror showed Alice they could have been identical twins. She was amazed Harry hadn't spotted it.

So all Alice had to do was to get in the cage! It would save a lot of time and explanation. Sophie would find *her*, and realise immediately something weird had happened. Alice thought she'd be safer in there, anyway.

Harry was still whittering on with his complaints. Alice took no notice, and started checking out the cage door. It was made of bars, like the rest of the cage, and kept shut by a hook that dropped into a metal ring.

Alice thought she might be able to push it up with her snout. She stood on her hind legs, stuck her snout under it, and strained with every bit of her strength... until finally the hook popped up and the door sprang open.

'I'm coming in, Harry, OK?' she said.

'Please yourself,' said Harry as Alice landed on the chippings. 'But *I'm* not staying in this hell-hole for hamsters a second longer.'

With that, Harry leapt out of the cage and headed for the kitchen.

'Harry, stop!' Alice shouted.

'Not likely!' he replied, and did a joyful little skip. 'I'm free! I'm free!'

Alice thought about going after him, then saw something that made her change her mind. A menacing shape appeared in the kitchen doorway.

Sinbad had recovered. And he looked pretty cross, too...

CHAPTER SEVEN
Too Loud, Too Slow

In fact, he was definitely furious, thought Alice. His yellow eye scanned the hall carpet like a spotlight searching for an escaped prisoner. And it wasn't long before it came to rest on the small, scurrying figure of... Harry.

For a second, Alice thought Harry was going to run straight into Sinbad's waiting claws. But Harry must have felt he was being watched.

He stopped in his tracks and looked upwards.

'Eeek!' he squeaked, faintly.

'So, you thought that was funny, did you, me getting bashed?' hissed Sinbad. Even at a distance Alice could see a large bump on his head.

'I d-d-don't know what you're t-t-talking about,' said Harry, terrified.

'There's no point in lying, Harry,' growled Sinbad. 'I heard you giggling. Still, you won't be doing much laughing when I've finished with you.'

Alice looked on, hopelessly. There was nothing she could do. Harry was about to be eaten, and it would be

her fault. If she hadn't let him out, he wouldn't be next to that space under the stairs, in mortal danger.

The space under the stairs... Alice realised it would be the perfect hiding place for a hamster on the run! Maybe Harry could get into a boot or a bag. It was so cluttered in there that Sinbad might never find him.

'To your right, Harry!' Alice yelled. 'Head for cover!'

Harry heard her, and glanced to his right. He must have seen what Alice meant. He didn't have to be told twice, anyway. He swung round, then dived into the deeper darkness beneath the giant hanging coats.

Now it was Sinbad's turn to be confused. He peered in Alice's direction, probably wondering who had called out, she thought. She ducked and hid in the chippings, not wanting the cat to know she was in Harry's cage.

Especially as the door was still wide open.

Alice held her breath and waited for Sinbad to make his move. But when he did, it wasn't what she was expecting. He cocked his head as if he were listening to something, then backed into the kitchen.

Phew, thought Alice. She had no time to relax, though. She heard voices and movement above her, and realised that was why Sinbad had gone. He wouldn't have wanted to be caught in the act.

Somebody was coming down the stairs, *CLUMP! CLUMP! CLUMP!*, and with every *CLUMP!* the cage

jumped. Alice craned her neck to look upwards, and saw two giants heading straight for her.

It was Sophie's mum, with Sophie behind her!

Sophie's mum reached the cage first, and bent over it, plunging it into shadow. She straightened again, and Alice noticed she was holding the huge letters the giant postman had delivered earlier.

Sophie, meanwhile, had immediately knelt down by the cage, shut the door with a loud *CLANG!* and firmly pushed the hook back into its ring. Then she put her enormous face up against the bars and started talking.

Alice gaped at her giant friend in amazement.

She couldn't understand a single word Sophie was saying.

It was like listening to a tape that was being played too loud, and far too slow. Alice concentrated her hardest, but it was no use. And when *she* tried talking to Sophie, she realised Sophie didn't understand *her*, either.

Alice couldn't believe she'd been so stupid. Of course she and Sophie couldn't talk to each other now! It was only in children's books that animals and people had conversations. This was real life.

She'd just have to come up with a different way to communicate, that was all. Perhaps she could use bits of Harry's food to write *HELP!* somewhere, like ship-wrecked sailors did with rocks on desert islands...

Suddenly Alice heard loud rattling directly above

her. Sophie had risen from her knees and was lifting the cage by its handle. Alice staggered as the cage swayed, and felt sick as it rose with terrifying speed into the air.

Sophie's mum unlatched the front door, and Sophie went outside with the cage. The Farr family estate car was waiting for them, its rear door open.

In all the excitement, Alice had forgotten about *The Roadshow*...

CHAPTER EIGHT
Nuts And Raisins

Sophie carefully put the cage containing Alice into the back of the car. She moved out of Alice's viewing range, and Sophie's mum shut the rear door with a *SLAM!* that shook the cage and knocked Alice off her paws.

Alice struggled to stand up, then heard other doors being opened and closed, the clicking of seatbelts, and the engine cough-coughing into life. She felt the cage floor throb, and the car turning into the road.

She soon discovered she was in for a pretty wild ride. Harry's cage vibrated continually. It *BOUNCED!* whenever the car hit any kind of bump, and slid alarmingly every time they went round a corner.

All Alice could do was hang on, and hope they weren't going the long way. After a few minutes, she was relieved to feel the car slowing down. It stopped, and the cage slid into the back seat with a... *DONK!*

The engine was still running, though. Alice wondered why, just as the car slowly moved forward again. Then it stopped once more. Maybe they were in a traffic jam... but then maybe they were queuing for a car park!

If they were, Alice knew she *had* to use this breathing space. Now was the moment to try out her desert-island signal idea. If she could only make Sophie pause for a second and think, she might get through to her...

Alice sat in the middle of Harry's cage and examined her surroundings.

A water bottle was attached to the bars on one side. Below it was a bowl filled with nuts and raisins. On the other side was an exercise wheel, and behind that, a ladder leading to a small sleeping platform.

The bottom of the cage was filled with a layer of chippings and bits of straw. Alice scuffled at it with her paws, revealing a patch of blue metal floor beneath. Great, she thought. It was exactly what she needed.

Alice went into action. She scrabbled as much of the floor clear as she could, piling up the chippings and straw round the edges of the cage. Then she started putting together a message made out of Harry's food.

It was harder than she'd expected. The food was easy enough to hold and carry. Her hamster paws and mouth were perfectly designed for the job. But getting the nuts and raisins into position was something else.

The 'H' was OK. But Alice had to keep walking across it to make the 'E' and the 'L', and it was hard to know where her rear paws were treading. She should have started with the 'P' and gone backwards, she thought.

The car crept forward every so often, too. Whenever it did, loose chippings and bits of straw fell back onto the clear patch. Alice had to remove them without disturbing the work she had already done.

But she finished at last. Then she climbed quickly up the ladder to the sleeping platform for a better look at the completed message.

'Not bad, though I do say so myself,' she murmured, proudly. 'I can't wait to see the look on Sophie's face when she gets an eyeful of that.'

But suddenly, Alice felt the car jerk forward and begin to pick up speed. Then there was a colossal... BUMP! that sent Alice's message leaping high off the floor, and launched *her* from the sleeping platform.

There was another *BUMP!*, and another, and another, *BUMP! BUMP!* The car rocked, and pitched, and dipped. By the time it came to a final halt, Alice was lying in a tangled heap of chippings, straw and food.

She was very cross. All her hard work had gone for absolutely nothing. And at that moment, she didn't even know which end of her was up.

She did hear Sophie and her parents getting out of the car, though, and the rear door being opened. Alice scrabbled frantically, and managed to poke her head from the tangle just as Sophie grabbed the cage handle.

Alice knew what was coming this time, and didn't feel quite so sick as the cage rose dizzyingly out of the

car. But she wasn't prepared for the noise. A tidal wave of sound suddenly crashed over her.

Alice gripped the cage bars, and peered through, trembling. Engines roared, horns toot-tooted, and people shouted. Before her was a chaos of massive cars parking and giants careering around.

And Sophie was taking her right into the heart of it.

CHAPTER NINE

A Missed Appointment

Alice panicked, and immediately ducked back into the tangle of chippings and straw. Her first instinct was to hide from the terrifying chaos outside. Then she realised that behaving like a *real* hamster wouldn't help.

It certainly wouldn't change anything.

OK, her desert-island plan had failed miserably. But Alice was still convinced she could communicate with somebody, somehow. She just had to stay alert and an opportunity would present itself, she thought.

So Alice swallowed hard, took a deep breath, and poked her head up again. She peered cautiously through the bars, and simply concentrated on *not* being frightened. It worked, and soon she felt much calmer.

She began to make sense of what had happened, too. Sophie and her parents *had* been queuing for a car park. But it was a temporary one in the corner of the park where *The Roadshow* would be taking place.

That explained the bumping, thought Alice. Once they'd come off the road and started driving across the grass, they must have gone over lots of ruts and ridges and holes. It had been a very dry summer.

Now Sophie was walking with her parents down a path between the parked cars and some trees. Alice knew the trees formed a small wood that separated the main area of the park from the swings and round-abouts.

Sophie had been right about it being crowded today, thought Alice. It seemed as if practically every family in the town had turned up for *The Roadshow*, and they were all heading in the same direction.

Alice caught a glimpse of a huge banner in the distance with the words *Kids Rule OK!* on it, but then her view was blocked. People jostled against the cage, and she had to move back from the bars.

Eventually, Sophie and her parents stepped out of the heaving mass and stopped in a clear space. They stood near some barriers with Alice, while the other giants continued to flow through a gap under the banner.

Alice glanced up at Sophie and her parents. Sophie

was scanning the crowd, and seemed anxious. Then Alice realised Sophie was looking for *her*. After all, they *had* arranged to meet at *The Roadshow* entrance!

It gave Alice an odd feeling to know Sophie was waiting for her to turn up, when in fact she was already there in the cage. Alice thought about trying to attract Sophie's attention, but she knew it would be useless.

This was an appointment Alice was definitely going to miss.

Sophie and her parents obviously didn't want to miss *The Roadshow*, though. They waited a while, did some talking during which Sophie's Mum and Dad

pointed at the crowd, then the Farr family went in, too.

Alice realised Sophie's parents had probably said they wouldn't be able to see her with so many people around, and that she might have gone in, anyway. It *was* the most logical thing to assume, thought Alice.

To her relief, the crowd thinned out beyond the barriers, although she could see it thickened again a bit further on. For a few seconds, she had a great view of *The Roadshow*... and she was very impressed.

It was familiar from the TV, of course, but better. There was a stage built on scaffolding, with a huge TV screen at the back, banks of speakers at the sides, and a

central area where the presenters did their stuff.

Alice glimpsed a couple of men with cameras, and a woman who kept shouting and waving her arms. *And there was Johnny Dee!*

Alice was thrilled... but then the feeling fizzled away, and she sank into gloom. This should have been the most exciting day of her life. But she couldn't enjoy it because she had been turned into... *a hamster!*

A young woman with a clipboard came over, spoke to Sophie, and looked at Alice. There was more talking, then the young woman led Sophie and her parents through another set of barriers, and behind the stage.

Alice suddenly worked out what was going on. The young woman had chosen *her*, Alice Buggins, to be in the Pet Talent Contest! And that meant Alice was about to appear live on TV to *millions* of people.

It could be just the opportunity she'd been waiting for...

CHAPTER TEN

Show Business

Alice's wait wasn't over yet, though. The young woman with the clipboard led Sophie and her parents to one of *The Roadshow* vans, and took them in. Alice saw that it was packed full of pet contestants and their owners.

Sophie put the cage on the floor. Then the woman Alice had seen shouting outside came into the van. She called all the owners together to listen to her at one end. Most of the pets were left where they were.

Alice was glad not to be swinging through the air any more, and just sat still for a moment. Then she heard a strange snuffling, and sniffed a rather unpleasant whiff. She looked up – and squeaked with surprise.

A colossal dog was watching her through the roof of the cage. Gigantic folds of skin hung from his jaws, and a huge loop of drool looked dangerously as if it were on the point of dropping from his mouth.

'Touch of stage fright, sweetie?' drawled the dog, his bad breath beating down on Alice with every word. 'I can always tell, especially with anyone new like you. I'll bet this is your very first talent contest, isn't it?'

'Er... yes,' said Alice, keeping a wary eye on the drool.

'I *thought* I'd never seen you before,' said another voice, suspiciously. Alice lowered her gaze to a second, smaller dog, who seemed to be covered in ribbons. 'What *exactly* will you be doing?' the dog snapped.

'I wish I knew,' sighed Alice, barely noticing she was speaking fluent dog. All that mattered was coming up with a way to use the opportunity she'd been given. But her brain seemed completely dead.

'Well, you'd better not decide to take up singing,' said the second dog, narrowing her eyes menacingly. 'Not if you want to stay healthy, that is.'

'Relax, Fifi,' said the first dog. 'I don't think this little chap will be any competition for us old troupers. I'm sure he's simply glad to be involved in show business.

The audience, the applause, the glamour...'

Alice stared at him. Her brain had just come to life.

So this was *show* business, was it? In that case, maybe she ought to put on a little show of her own. She might not be able to *talk* to the rest of the human race – but that needn't stop her communicating, she thought...

'Actually, I think I know what I'm going to do now,' she said, confidently. 'But you needn't worry. It won't involve any singing.'

'That's the spirit!' said the first dog, turning to go. 'And remember, don't be *too* upset if you come last, sweetie. I know it's hard, but we all have to start somewhere. Next stop Hollywood, eh? Best of luck!'

Fifi just gave Alice a dirty look, and trotted off with

her snout snootily in the air. Alice wanted to say something cutting, but there was no time.

The woman must have stopped talking to the owners, because suddenly they came back to collect their pets. There was lots of bustling and shoving and shouting, then Sophie appeared and grabbed the cage handle.

Alice braced herself as the cage rose into the air. She couldn't see much, surrounded as she was by jostling giants, both human and animal. But that didn't matter. She had a pretty good idea where they were going.

They walked across an open space ringed by vans, climbed a few steps between some scaffolding poles... and emerged onto the stage. Alice had been expecting it to be daunting, but the reality was still a shock.

The noise was a thousand times worse than in the car park. Below her was a sea of faces, and Alice realised she was looking at the crowd that had come for *The Roadshow*. They were cheering and waving like mad.

She could hear *The Roadshow* theme tune, too. At least, that's what she thought it was. Rivers of sound were pouring out of the speakers, with a deep thudding bass line that made Alice's whole body judder.

The pets and their owners were ranged round the stage in a curve. Sophie had ended up on the extreme right. Alice could see Johnny Dee on the far side. He was holding a microphone, and talking to a cameraman.

The Pet Talent Contest was about to begin, and it was obvious Alice would be the last pet to perform. If only she had some fingers to cross...

Alice knew she would need every bit of luck she could get.

CHAPTER ELEVEN
What a Story!

Suddenly the music stopped pouring out of the speakers, and the crowd quietened down. Alice sat back on her hind legs and closed her eyes for a second. She had a human-sized headache in a hamster-sized skull.

When she opened her eyes again, she saw that Sophie was kneeling and staring at her through the cage bars. Sophie had the slightly worried expression on her face that Alice had seen so many times.

Then the crowd erupted once more, and Sophie stood up. Alice could see her looking across the stage, and heard Johnny Dee's voice booming from the speakers. The first pet must be performing, thought Alice.

She looked up at the giant TV screen behind her, and saw a boy holding a fat white rabbit. Johnny Dee was talking to it, and the cameraman had his lens almost touching the rabbit's nose, which kept twitching.

If that's what the rabbit's party piece was, then Alice wasn't very impressed. She could tell Johnny Dee wasn't, either. He moved on to the next pet, a plump guinea pig, and the next, and the next, and the next...

Alice knew the format. Every week, Johnny Dee went along the line of owners, cracking jokes. He watched what their pets could do, and the huge screen showed the crowd. Then he gave each pet a score out of ten.

Alice watched him coming closer, and closer, and closer...

None of the pets did anything remarkable. Two gerbils performed a sort of frantic trapeze act in their cage, and a snake tied itself in knots. Then a parrot did a few pathetic impersonations, and said something rude.

That seemed to cause a bit of a stir. But just wait until they saw what *she* was going to do, thought Alice. The idea made her laugh, inwardly. When she got going, the jaws of millions would drop in amazement...

Alice had simply decided to *act out* the things that had happened to her. She *knew* she could do it. It would be just like playing charades at Christmas, she reasoned, and she had always been utterly brilliant at that.

There were now only two pets left between Alice and Johnny Dee, the big drooling dog who had talked to Alice, and his mean friend, Fifi.

The drooling dog didn't do much except bark a lot, and Johnny Dee moved quickly on to Fifi. He held his microphone towards her, music blasted out of the speakers, and Fifi started singing. It was a terrible noise.

At least, *Alice* thought it sounded awful. Johnny Dee obviously liked it, for he gave Fifi ten out of ten, yelled

something which Alice realised must be 'Wow, knock-out!', threw his arms wide, and fell over backwards.

The crowd exploded. They were still laughing and cheering and clapping when he got to his feet and stood in front of Sophie and Alice.

A hush descended on the crowd as Johnny Dee talked to Sophie. Finally, Sophie bent to undo the cage door, gently grasped Alice, and eased her out. Then Sophie carefully placed her on the stage floor.

Alice looked up. Johnny Dee and his cameraman were squatting in front of her, with Sophie next to them, nervously chewing her lip. To Alice's left was the audience, and to her right, the huge TV screen.

She was startled to see a colossal hamster suddenly appear on it, but realised it was *her*, and that she was on live, nationwide television, too.

Alice took a deep breath... and gave it her best shot.

She acted out the whole story – and what a story it was! Getting up, walking to Sophie's house, the gas cloud descending, her transformation, the encounters with Sinbad and Harry, the journey to *The Roadshow*...

She stopped at last, completely puffed out, and waited for the reaction. But she soon saw Sophie's was the only jaw to have dropped. Sophie seemed absolutely stunned, while Johnny Dee just looked faintly amused.

He stood up, and Alice knew her chance was slipping away. She hadn't got through to them, and she had a feeling she never would – unless she did something dramatic now. She was desperate, but what could she do?

Then just as Johnny Dee was turning back to Fifi, it came to her. *Alice stood on her hind legs, threw her paws wide, and fell over backwards.*

What happened next was quite a surprise...

CHAPTER TWELVE

Despair

Johnny Dee whirled round and stared at Alice, who was still lying on her back. He spoke to the camera-man, and Alice realised he was talking about her. Perhaps he'd only seen part of what she'd done, she thought.

So to make sure, Alice scrambled to her paws... and did it again.

The crowd roared, and Alice could see that Johnny Dee was laughing. He threw his arms wide, and fell

over backwards himself. Then he jumped to his feet and came over to Sophie, who was still looking totally amazed.

Alice started to relax. She was convinced she'd got through to someone at last, and that Johnny Dee knew she wasn't what she seemed. No *ordinary* hamster would be able to copy his famous gimmick, after all.

Any second now, she thought, they'd take her somewhere and begin investigating. It would only be a question of time before the scientists worked out what had happened to her, and how to reverse it.

But then Alice felt herself being scooped up in Sophie's giant hands. Sophie held Alice close to her chest, with just her tiny head above the colossal fingers. Alice gulped, and felt dizzy. It was a long way down.

Johnny Dee's face loomed in front of her, and Alice saw him putting his arm round Sophie's shoulders. He slowly turned Sophie towards the rear of the stage, a deafening drum roll thundered out of the speakers...

And the words THE WINNER! flashed onto the huge TV screen.

The crowd went absolutely wild, but Alice took no notice. She didn't take any notice when Sophie gave her a gigantic, slobbery kiss, either, or when Sophie's parents rushed onto the stage and hugged their daughter.

Alice was filled with despair. She realised she *hadn't*

succeeded in getting through to anybody. As far as the rest of the human race was concerned, she was nothing more than a clever... *hamster.*

All she'd done by impersonating Johnny Dee was win Sophie the special prize, that fabulous trip for two with *The Roadshow* to Wonderworld. And that made being trapped in the body of a hamster much, much worse.

Alice was certain now she would never make it to Florida. No, she brooded as Sophie gently popped her back into the cage and left the stage, she would be spending the rest of her short, anonymous life behind bars.

Even when her Mum and Dad discovered she had gone missing and started searching for her, they wouldn't think to look *inside* Harry's cage. Besides, Alice had given up on the idea of communicating with people.

It seemed completely impossible, she thought numbly.

Sophie and her parents had stopped near one of the vans, and were talking to the young woman with the clipboard. Alice noticed that Sophie still looked anxious as well as pleased, and kept pointing at the cage.

Alice sighed, then lay down in the chippings and loose straw on the floor. She was very tired, and she was beginning to feel quite hungry, too.

'I suppose I'll have to get used to nuts and raisins,'

she muttered, although what she really fancied was a hamburger and fries. And when she realised she might never eat food like that again, she wanted to cry.

Suddenly, Alice felt the cage move. Sophie and her Dad seemed to be leaving the backstage area, while Sophie's Mum was staying behind. They made their way through the cheering crowd, and under the banner.

Alice told herself she didn't care what they did, but she couldn't help being puzzled about what was going on. Then she saw that Sophie and her Dad were heading for the car park, and everything fell into place.

Sophie and her parents had probably been invited to watch the rest of the show, thought Alice. But she

could tell from Sophie's face her friend was worried it had all been too much for a nervous hamster.

So Sophie was taking the cage back to the car to give her pet some peace and quiet. When they reached the car park, Sophie's Dad opened the car's rear door, Sophie put the cage in, and the door was shut with a *SLAM!*

Alice heard another door being opened, then an odd noise, and a door being closed. She looked up, but Sophie and her Dad had gone.

Then Alice saw something shimmering drifting past outside...

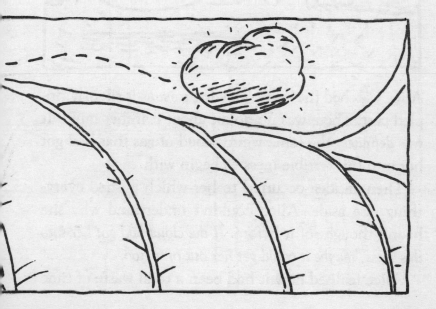

CHAPTER THIRTEEN
The Great Escape

Alice watched the eerily glowing mist as it silently rippled past. There was no doubt about it in her mind. It was *definitely* the same weird cloud òf gas that had got her into this terrible mess to begin with.

Then an idea occurred to her which pushed everything else aside. Alice couldn't understand why she hadn't thought of it before. *If the cloud had got her into this mess, maybe it could get her out of it, too.*

Alice realised now it had been a total waste of time

trying to communicate with anybody. No one would take notice of a hamster, for heaven's sake! She should simply have followed the gas cloud.

It had changed her once, so it might very well change her back. All she had to do was to let the cloud touch her while she was thinking of herself the way she had been – a proper human being, and not a hamster!

Alice relaxed, pleased she'd actually managed to think of a solution to her problem. She saw the last wisps of the gas cloud wafting by the car's rear window, and thought she had better go after it.

Then Alice experienced a familiar, sinking feeling as she realised that might not be such an easy thing to do. Getting out of Harry's cage wouldn't be very difficult. She would just do the same as when she had got in.

But how the heck was she going to get out of the car?

The doors were bound to be locked. Alice was sure she wouldn't be able to operate the handles, anyway. They would probably be almost as big as her, and far too stiff to move with her tiny hamster paws.

Then Alice remembered that odd noise, and wondered if it might have been the sound of Sophie unwinding a window a little. Sophie wouldn't have wanted the car to get too stuffy while the cage was in it...

Alice shot up the ladder to the sleeping platform, stood on her hind legs, and peered through the bars. With some straining, she could just see over the back

seat. And good old Sophie *had* left a window slightly open!

There was no time to lose. Alice scampered down the ladder and over to the cage door. She stuck her snout under the hook, and pushed at it with all her strength. It popped out of the ring, and the door swung wide.

Next, Alice jumped to a wheel arch, and from there she scrambled to the top of the back seat. Then she ran

along it, a bit like a circus performer on a high wire, and made it to the window that was open.

There wasn't a big gap, but it was enough. Alice climbed up a seat belt and put one front paw on the glass. Then she squeezed her head and another paw through, and wriggled round to grab the edge of the roof.

Her grip nearly slipped... but she scrabbled frantically, and hung on.

Gradually she eased her body through, and pulled herself further and further

out. At last, with a few kicks from her rear paws, the
great escape was complete, and
Alice was on the roof of the
car, panting.

She could just see the
cloud of gas moving
slowly towards the
trees. She ran
across the roof and
stopped where the

windscreen began. She slid down it, dashed over the
bonnet, took a deep breath... and jumped.

She landed with a
THUMP! on the hard,
dry ground, and rolled
over. She didn't pause,
though. She scuttled
over the brittle, brown
grass, under a car, then
another, and another,
and emerged onto the
path.

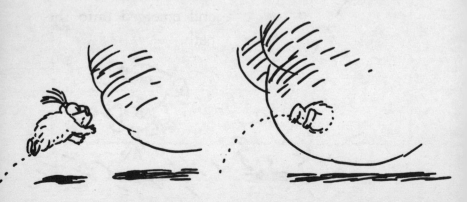

The cloud was floating through the small wood and towards the playground. Alice dashed after it, glad no one seemed to be around. She didn't want anybody to prevent her from doing what she had to.

Alice lost sight of the cloud in the shadows under the trees, and hoped the breeze she could feel wouldn't make it impossible to catch. But the cloud was there in the playground when she came out into the sunlight.

It was floating past the swings, and Alice put on a final spurt.

She remembered to fill her mind with images of what she used to be, what she so badly wanted to be again – ordinary Alice Buggins, a girl with arms and legs and all the other bits and pieces a human being should have.

Then she plunged into the cloud's shimmering coils.

CHAPTER FOURTEEN
Alice's Secret

Alice closed her eyes as the glowing mist swirled round her. She expected to be struck by that strange feeling in the stomach, but it didn't happen. Instead, the terrible tingling came first, and it started with her ears.

GNIP! GNIP! they suddenly went, and her nose went *POP!* backwards. Then the tingling tickled her cheeks, crackled down her neck, flowed over her body, raced down her legs, and finally reached her paws.

Alice realised she had gone rigid from top to bottom.

She fell over onto her side, her limbs sticking out stiffly. It was then that a strange sensation invaded her stomach – but it was very different from before.

This time, Alice felt as if she were actually being pumped up from somewhere in her middle. There was no other way to describe it. Every part of her tiny body seemed to be expanding relentlessly from inside.

She squeaked, and she squealed, and she gritted her teeth. The pumping grew stronger, and stronger, and stronger, and Alice thought that if it went on much longer, she wouldn't be able to stand it any more.

Eventually there was a loud TWANG!, and four crisp cracks, CRACK! CRACK! CRACK! CRACK!... then everything went rather quiet. Alice was dazed and dizzy, although she remembered that would soon pass.

It did. But she hardly dared to open her eyes.

She knew she had to. She cautiously opened one, and squinted down. She couldn't see any orange fur or pink paws, so she carefully opened her other eye, and gave her entire body a thorough looking over.

Alice breathed a *huge* sigh of relief. She was back to normal!

She was standing near the swings, and there was no sign of the weird gas cloud. It seemed to have disappeared. Good riddance, thought Alice. She wanted to jump for joy now she was her old self again.

She could hear music and cheering in the distance, and realised *The Roadshow* was still in progress. There was nothing to stop her from going to watch it, either! She was a person, just like anyone else.

Alice ran out of the playground gate and down the path towards *The Roadshow*. It was great having long, *human* legs once more, and not being forced to scurry around on those pathetic little paws.

Mind you, she thought, it had been a pretty fantastic experience.

'Wait till I tell Sophie,' she murmured as she approached the barriers. 'She'll be *so* jealous that I've been a hamster, and she hasn't.'

Alice suddenly stopped short, and thought about what she'd said. She pictured herself telling Sophie and her own Mum and Dad that she'd been turned into a hamster by a gas cloud, then back into a girl.

They simply wouldn't believe it! She might be able to convince Sophie, but Alice knew that convincing grown-ups was a completely different matter. They'd probably think she had just gone totally crazy.

Then Alice realised she might not want them to believe her... If they did, she would almost certainly be whipped into hospital, or some secret scientific laboratory where she'd be subjected to loads of experiments.

She had seen too many episodes of the *X-Files* to be happy about that idea. Either way, *she* would lose out, Alice thought, grimly. *Especially if it meant she wouldn't be allowed to visit Wonderworld with Sophie.*

Alice hadn't forgotten about winning the prize. And she wasn't going to let it slip from her grasp, not after all she'd suffered. The whole incredible adventure would simply have to stay her secret – forever.

Still, it would have been nice to tell somebody, thought Alice. But a free trip to the best theme park in Florida was definitely worth her silence.

She went under the banner and into the crowd. She

made straight for the entrance to the backstage area, hoping she would see Sophie, and that she could get in to meet Johnny Dee – as a human being, this time!

Alice couldn't help smiling at the memory of the look on Sophie's face while she had been acting out her story. Sophie could never have expected Harry to come up with anything like that. Then Alice's smile vanished.

Oh no, she thought. *What about Harry?*

CHAPTER FIFTEEN

Hang On, Harry!

Alice! *Alice, over here,*' someone shouted at her from behind a barrier. Alice looked round and saw Sophie waving. 'So you finally managed to show up!' Sophie added as Alice approached. 'Where have you *been?*'

'Er, sorry... it was my Mum and Dad's fault,' said Alice, suddenly thinking of a terrific alibi. 'They couldn't bring me because they're ill...'

'Never mind, that's not important,' said Sophie. Alice could see she was bubbling with excitement. 'Did you watch any of it on TV?' Sophie asked. Alice shook her head. 'You didn't? Well, have I got a surprise for *you...*'

Alice listened while Sophie told her what she already knew. Pretending she *didn't* know was Alice's second brilliant performance of the day. And pretending she was pleased and excited was her third.

Part of her was delighted, she had to admit. But the pleasure was over-shadowed. Gruesome, blood-spattered images of what might be happening to Harry *at that very moment* kept intruding into Alice's thoughts.

She *had* to get back to Sophie's house as quickly as possible.

'I don't want to spoil your day, Sophie,' said Alice, breaking into her friend's chatter at last. 'But do you think we could leave... *now?*'

'I don't understand,' said Alice, puzzled. 'Wouldn't you like to come over and meet Johnny Dee? I thought you were his biggest fan.'

'I am,' said Alice. 'I just don't feel very well. I think I'm coming down with the same tummy bug as my Mum and Dad. Besides... I'll be meeting Johnny Dee on the trip to Florida. You *will* be taking me, won't you?'

'Of *course* I will, silly,' said Sophie, looking concerned. Alice clutched her tummy. 'I would never even have dreamed of doing this if it hadn't been for you,' said Sophie. 'Wait here while I get my Mum and Dad...'

Soon Sophie, her parents and Alice were heading for the car park. When they arrived at the car, Sophie peered in and suddenly looked rather anxious. With a jolt, Alice realised *the cage was empty*.

'Poor old Harry!' said Alice, thinking fast. 'It's all been a bit much for him. He must be snuggled in that tangle, snoring his head off. He deserves a holiday...' she added, steering Sophie towards her seat.

'I hope he's OK,' said Sophie, glancing over her shoulder at the cage.

'He's fine,' said Alice, firmly. 'Now, tell me what he did again...'

Alice got Sophie talking about *The Roadshow* to distract her attention. Sophie's parents joined in, and Alice discovered they all believed her 'impersonation' of Johnny Dee had been a complete fluke.

Charming, thought Alice. But she couldn't put them right.

'I'll drop you off first then, shall I, Alice?' said Sophie's Mum.

'Actually, I'm feeling a lot better,' said Alice, hurriedly. 'So can I spend the rest of the morning with Sophie? I'm pretty sure my Mum and Dad could do with having the house to themselves for a bit longer...'

'Of course you can, Alice,' said Sophie's Dad.

Alice smiled sweetly, but inside she was a quivering,

nervous wreck. Hang on, Harry, she thought, and crossed her fingers. *Just hang on.*

She was the first one out of the car when they stopped, and hovered by the rear door. Sophie's Mum opened it, and Alice grabbed the cage. She put her arms round it to conceal as much of the interior as she could.

'Why don't you go and turn the TV on?' she said to Sophie. 'I'll take Harry up to your room, and then we can watch *The Roadshow* together.'

'OK,' said Sophie, and followed her parents through the front door.

Alice went in too, and waited till she had the hall to herself. Then she put the cage down, dashed to the space under the stairs... and saw Sinbad. He was just reaching into a shopping bag, but Alice beat him to it.

She found a small, furry bundle tightly curled up in a corner. It was Harry, and he was... still alive! He was also deeply asleep. Alice was so relieved, she held him up and gently kissed his warm little head.

'What was that you said about life not being fair, Sinbad?' she laughed.

But Sinbad... *didn't say a word.*

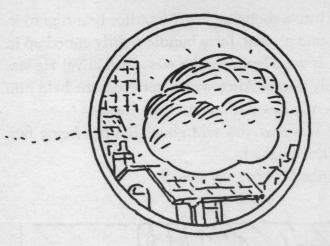

*A small cloud of gas floats away from a noisy park...
It shimmers, and gives off an eerie glow.
Where it will drift next is a mystery. Perhaps it
will waft its way silently into the country.
Perhaps it will come coiling down another quiet
street... whatever the truth, one thing is
certain. Whoever meets it is in for an amazing
experience, as one girl discovered. And next
time, it might be you tumbling into the weird, wild
and wonderful world of...* **Swoppers!**

PHEW!
I'M WHACKED
AFTER
THAT!